AF270367

Weather of the Rain Forest

by Julie Murray

Dash!
LEVELED READERS
An Imprint of Abdo Zoom • abdobooks.com

Level 1 – Beginning
Short and simple sentences with familiar words or patterns for children who are beginning to understand how letters and sounds go together.

Level 2 – Emerging
Longer words and sentences with more complex language patterns for readers who are practicing common words and letter sounds.

Level 3 – Transitional
More developed language and vocabulary for readers who are becoming more independent.

abdobooks.com

Published by Abdo Zoom, a division of ABDO, PO Box 398166, Minneapolis, Minnesota 55439.
Copyright © 2023 by Abdo Consulting Group, Inc. International copyrights reserved in all countries.
No part of this book may be reproduced in any form without written permission from the publisher.
Dash!™ is a trademark and logo of Abdo Zoom.

Printed in the United States of America, North Mankato, Minnesota.
102022
012023

Photo Credits: Getty Images, Shutterstock
Production Contributors: Kenny Abdo, Jennie Forsberg, Grace Hansen, John Hansen
Design Contributors: Candice Keimig, Neil Klinepier

Library of Congress Control Number: 2022937230

Publisher's Cataloging in Publication Data

Names: Murray, Julie, author.
Title: Weather of the rain forest / by Julie Murray
Description: Minneapolis, Minnesota : Abdo Zoom, 2023 | Series: Rain forest life | Includes online resources and index.
Identifiers: ISBN 9781098280130 (lib. bdg.) | ISBN 9781098280666 (ebook) | ISBN 9781098280963 (Read-to-Me ebook)
Subjects: LCSH: Tropics--Climate--Juvenile literature. | Tropical meteorology--Juvenile literature. | Rain forests--Juvenile literature. | Temperate rain forest ecology--Juvenile literature.
Classification: DDC 577.34--dc23

Table of Contents

Weather of the Rain Forest

What do rain, **humidity**, snow, and fog have in common? They are all types of weather found in rain forests around the world!

Tropical vs. Temperate

6

There are two types of rain forests. There are **tropical** and **temperate** rain forests.

They are in different areas of the world. They also have different weather.

Tropical rain forests are found near the **equator**. It is hot and **humid** all year long.

Temperatures range between 70° and 85° Fahrenheit (21° and 30° C).

It rains almost every day. It
can rain up to 400 inches
(1,000 cm) a year!

Temperate rain forests are found in cooler areas farther from the **equator**. They are mainly along coasts.

Temperatures in **temperate** rain forests are mild. They range from 32° to 68° Fahrenheit (0° to 20° C). It can get cold enough to snow!

These forests are often
foggy. They can have up to
200 inches (500 cm) of rain
a year.

- The Amazon rainforest is the largest **tropical** rain forest. It covers about half of South America!

- Alaska's Tongass National Forest is the largest **temperate** rain forest in the world.

- Rain forests experience natural disasters such as floods, **droughts**, landslides, and forest fires.

Glossary

drought – a long period with little or no rain.

equator – the imaginary circle around the middle of the earth that is halfway between the North and South Poles.

humid – having a high amount of water vapor; damp.

humidity – the state of being humid.

temperate – having neither extremely hot nor extremely cold temperatures and mild weather.

tropical – having a climate in which there is no frost and where plants can grow all year long.

Index

Online Resources